My First Prayer Book

Text
Sr. Karen Cavanagh, CSJ

Cover Illustration
William Luberoff

Text Illustrations
Edward Letwenko

Regina Press

New York

Copyright © 1998 by The Regina Press.
All rights reserved. No part of this book
may be reproduced in any form without
expressed permission from the publisher.
Cover artwork copyright © 1998 by Reproducta Inc.

JESUS LEARNED TO PRAY AS A CHILD

PRAYER:
Jesus, You are my teacher. Teach me the love of God and the love of prayer which You learned and taught to Your friends and followers. Amen.

The Prayer Jesus Taught His Friends

Our Father

Our Father, who are in heaven,
hallowed be thy name;
thy kingdom come;
thy will be done on earth as it is in heaven.
Give us this day our daily bread;
and forgive us our trespasses
as we forgive those who trespass against us;
and lead us not into temptation,
but deliver us from evil. Amen.

Prayer As Day Begins

PRAYER:
God of love, today is another beginning. I give to You everything I will do, say and be today. Be with me. I am Your child and I love You. Amen.

A Prayer Before Eating — Grace Before Meals

PRAYER:
Bless us God and bless this food which comes from Your goodness. May it make us healthy and strong. Amen.

A Prayer Of Faith

PRAYER:
God, I believe in You and in Your goodness. I believe You have given me life and that You share Your life with me. You share it with the gift of Jesus and the Spirit whom You give me. I believe that You made me to know You and love You. Thank you for Your gift of faith. Amen.

A Prayer Of Hope

PRAYER:
God, I know You keep promises and so I trust You. I trust You will always care for me and will forgive me when I am not loving. Help me to know You more and more and to be more like You. Amen.

A Prayer Of Love

PRAYER:
God of wonder and love, all of me loves You. I love You with my heart and my mind and my body. Because of Your love I can show my love to other people. Please help me to be a loving person. Amen.

A Prayer Of Praise

PRAYER:
God, You are great and wonderful! Angels and children and all of Your people praise You. When I look at the sky and the stars and the moon I am so filled with praise. You care so much for us, that You created us like Yourself and gave us this world. Amen.

A Prayer About School

PRAYER:
God, sometimes it's hard to be in school each day. I give You all my school work and homework and ask You to bless it. Help me to work well and study hard so that I will learn the things that will help me in life. Amen.

A Prayer For My Teacher

PRAYER:
Bless my teacher, God, for spending so much time with me. Give my teacher patience, love and understanding and help me to be a good student. Jesus, You are the best of teachers. Please be with my teacher. Amen.

A Prayer For My Friends

PRAYER:
Jesus, You had many friends and You cared for them at all times. Thank You for my friends and all they do for me. Help me to be a good friend, to play fair and to show care to all my friends. Please take care of them. Amen.

A Prayer For Mothers

PRAYER:
God, mothers are like You because they give us life and care for us with their lives. Bless my mother and all mothers with Your love. Help me to love her the way she loves me. Amen.

A Prayer For Fathers

PRAYER:
Fathers are like You, God, as they provide for their children. God, take care of my dad. Help him to know my love and how much I need his love. When I grow up I want to be his friend. Amen.

A Prayer For Brothers And Sisters

PRAYER:
Thank You, God, for my brothers and sisters. With them I learn to be part of a family. Help us to share and to live in peace in our home. Teach us to be forgiving when we fight or hurt each other. Give us much love. Amen.

GOD, MASTER OF

When I listen to God I pray. When I think abo[ut]
think about the kind of person God wants me [to be]
me to be I pray. God, teach me to pray!

All The Universe

od I pray. When I talk to God I pray. When I
e I pray. When I am the boy or girl God wants

A Prayer For Grandparents

PRAYER:
Grandparents make children feel so special, God. They always have time and so many stories to tell. Take good care of my grandparents and all older people. Dear God, help them to always be loving, patient and special. Amen.

A Prayer For Forgiveness

PRAYER:
God of all love, sometimes I am selfish and unloving as I speak and behave. Sometimes I disobey or am mean to others. I am so sorry when I offend you and hurt others. Forgive me and help me please to start all over. Amen.

A Prayer In Spring

PRAYER:
God, You make the world so colorful after the long, cold winter. Thank You for flowers and singing birds and all the wonderful gifts of spring which show Your love. Let me always see You in nature. Amen.

A Prayer At Easter

PRAYER:
God, You brought Jesus, Your Son, to new life. Give me His new life, too. What love You have for me. Help me to be faithful to Your life which You gave to me at baptism. Amen.

A Prayer In Summer

PRAYER:
In the summer I can see and touch Your love, God. I see it in the sky and the sun and the water. I feel it in the warmth and touch of sunshine and playmates. Thank You for this time and for the beautiful world. Amen.

A Prayer For Pets

PRAYER:
You care for all creatures, God, and You ask me to do the same. Thank You for my pet and for all animals. Every fish and dog, every kitten and hamster, every bird and turtle is Your work of art. I praise You. Amen.

A Prayer In Autumn

PRAYER:
The leaves are falling, God, and it's getting dark so early. It reminds me that I must quiet down and think of You and Your goodness. You give me every day and are with me in the bright and the dark times of my life. May I never forget. Amen.

A Prayer For Thanksgiving

PRAYER:
Today is a special day for giving thanks, God. You give me every good thing and I forget at times to thank You. For family and health, for friends and food, for love and Your life I thank You, thank You, thank You. Amen.

A Prayer In Winter

PRAYER:
God of all seasons, grown-ups think snow is a nuisance but I love it. Every snowflake is special and different. Let them remind me of how special and wonderful You have created each of us. Help me to always see the good in every person. Amen.

A Prayer At Christmas

PRAYER:
God, You gave us the greatest gift of all — Jesus. At Christmas time I remember this love. Thank You for Jesus. Help me to keep this gift in mind when I see so many other Christmas gifts. Let me give others the gift of love. Amen.

A Prayer For A Sick Person

PRAYER:
God, You care for everyone. Please give health to people who are sick and help them to be patient with their sickness. Give special blessings to the people who take care of them. Let them know Your love and healing. Amen.

A Prayer After Eating — Grace After Meals

PRAYER:
We give You thanks, God, for this food and all the blessings which we have received from Your goodness. May we always remember the people who are poor and hungry. Help us to share Your gifts. Amen.

A Prayer As The Day Ends

PRAYER:
God of peace, thank You for another day and all that was in it. Forgive me for any wrong I have done and give me Your love. Bless my parents, my family and all who care for me. Keep me in Your care this night and help me to love You more tomorrow. Amen.

WE BEGIN AND END ALL OUR PRAYER

In the name of the Father, and of the Son, and of the Holy Spirit. Amen.

My Own Special Prayer

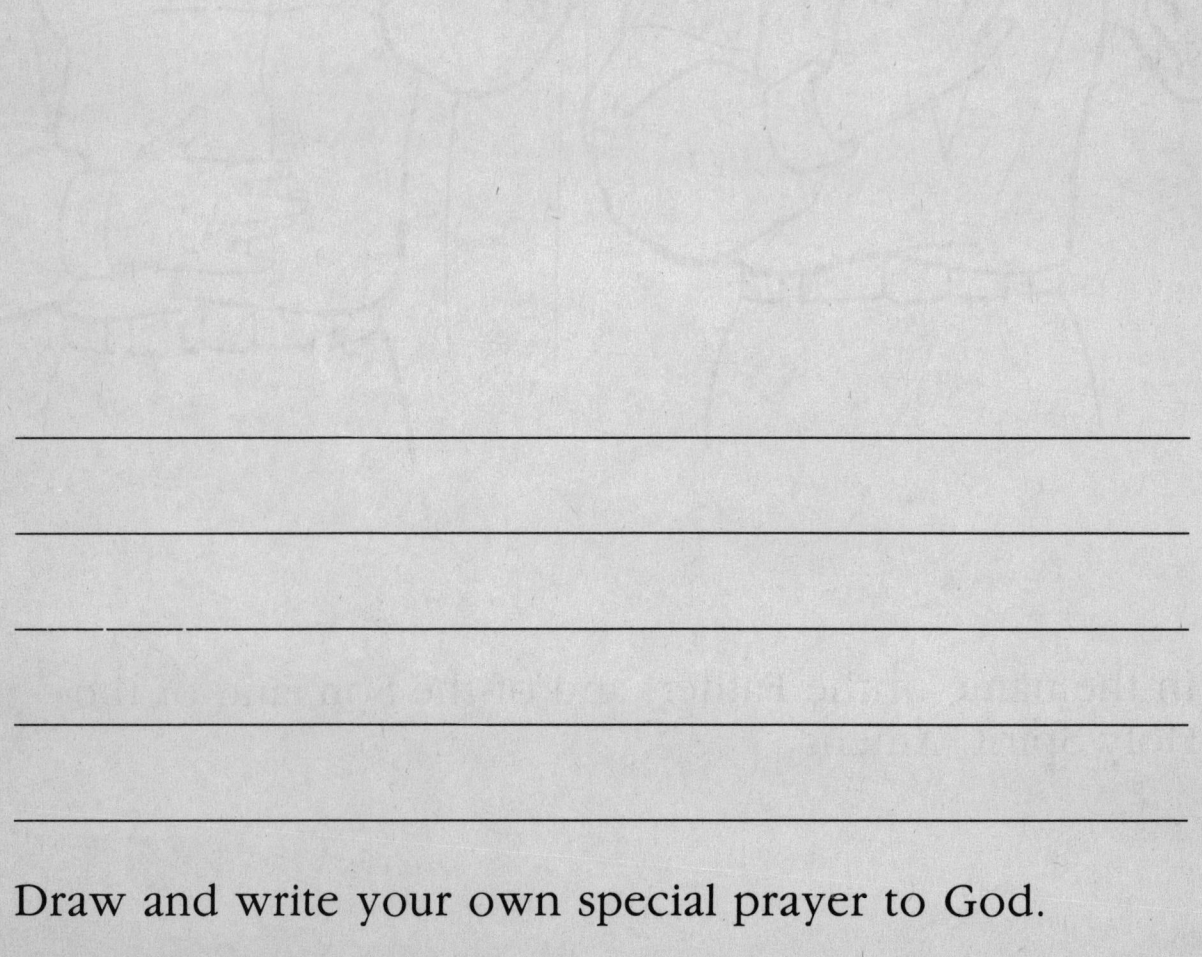

_____

_____

_____

_____

_____

Draw and write your own special prayer to God.